Tap Dancing

By Heather Hammonds

Tap dancing is a special way to dance.

Tap dancers
have special shoes.

The shoes have taps
on the heels and the toes.

Tap shoes make
a tapping sound.

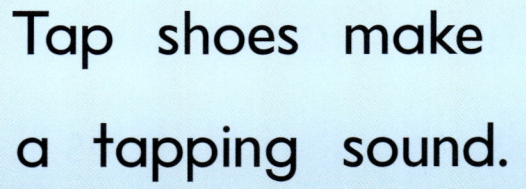

Tap dancers tap their feet to the music.

Tap dancers tap
to fast music.

Tap dancers tap
to slow music, too.

Tap dancers dance
in shows.

They dance in movies, too.

Children learn to tap dance at a dance school.

A teacher shows the children the dance.

The children learn to dance to the music.

Tap dancing is fun.